Redemption
Reconciliation
Righteousness
Rejoicing and
Refreshing

Rev. Betty Hargis Kemper

Copyright © 2020

Rev. Betty Jean Hargis Kemper

Printed in USA

Scripture quotations marked (KJV) are taken from the King James Version of the Bible.

Scripture quotations marked (AMP) are taken from the Amplified Bible, Copyright © 1954, 1958, 1962, 1964, 1965, 1987 by The Lockman Foundation. Used by permission. (www.Lockman.org)

Scripture quotations marked (NIV) are taken from the Holy Bible, New International Version®, NIV®. Copyright © 1973, 1978, 1984, 2011 by Biblica, Inc.™ Used by permission of Zondervan. All rights reserved worldwide. www.zondervan.com The "NIV" and "New International Version" are trademarks registered in the United States Patent and Trademark Office by Biblica, Inc.

Table of Contents

Foreword

It is a great honor to write the foreword for my sister, Betty Jean's newest book. From childhood, Betty has had a steadfast passion to know and serve the Lord Jesus Christ and to follow His call on her life. Having her for my sister, prayer partner and confidante is a precious gift. Because of our closeness, I laughingly say that she and I were meant to be twins but I was so busy talking in Heaven that I missed that opportunity and had to wait for the next time.

Betty has a genuine love for people and gives generously of her time, talents, and resources to others in hospitality, in fervent prayers and ministering in any way that is needed. She has devoted her time to studying

God's word to better communicate the good news of the gospel and has published five other books.

I have walked with her as she has endeavored to share her stories in a biblical perspective. I am proud to be her sister and cheerleader. May you be blessed, encouraged, and have your faith strengthened as you read her book.

Debi Dye Martin
M. Ed. Early Childhood

Dedication

This book is dedicated to our precious Heavenly Father, Son and Holy Spirit. According to Psalm 78, parents are to teach the Bible to their children so they will know God, hope in God, and not forget the works of God but keep His commandments. Parents cannot afford to leave this job of teaching their children about God to our schools and colleges. From my college experience, they tried to teach me to depend on myself and others and not on God.

To answer this call to proclaim the gospel, I not only dedicate this book to my children and every generation after them, but also to you and your children to a thousand generations. May God use this book to bless all the children (young and old) in the United States of America and on every continent all around the world.

This book contains 5R's for knowing Christ more intimately. My prayer is that you and your children will enjoy this study on **redemption, reconciliation, righteousness, rejoicing and times of refreshing in the presence of the Lord.** There is a river that flows from the throne of God. Come on and wade in the water with me.

Introduction

Many years ago, I asked someone to write a book about the 5 R's. These are   gifts God has given to us by His Amazing Grace. When I did not get a response, I realized the Lord was encouraging me to write the book. I began writing years ago, but I had put this book aside. This morning I was having my "Come to Jesus" meeting. I heard His gentle voice prompting me to get back to writing this book. I said, "Lord, I repent and I will begin today."

When I am given instruction from the Lord or even being chastised, the Lord always speaks to me in a kind voice with such encouraging words of comfort to let me know I can do whatever he is telling me. According to scripture, God does chastise those he loves. You and I are loved by our Heavenly Father and He has equipped us for every good work. I always thank the Lord when we have our dialogues and I leave our place of communion with great joy.

I know He lives in me and is my hope of glory. When we have a relationship with Jesus, we must go deeper into our quiet times in order to hear His voice and become intimate with Him. Deep calls unto deep. I find supernatural peace when I am quiet as I commune with the Lord. Also, there is a precious, unique corporate anointing when we are in church with the saints.

The Bible says that we are His sheep and we hear His voice. My desire is to wake up every morning praising the Lord and communicating with Him as I receive the great plans He has for me for that day. Then I go forth with love, peace and joy in my heart. I rise up with great vitality from the oneness of being with my Heavenly Father. When I listen for His instructions for my pathway for the day, my whole day goes tremendously better.

I realize it is very important for me to be still, to listen and to obey the Lord. Check out my book, <u>SSSSSSSH! The Word of the Lord Shall Prevail</u>. In this book, I talk about a time when the Lord had to say to me, "Shut up, Betty." I knew He meant for me to be still and to remember that He is on the throne.

I know that the Lord is always with me; **until I stop and take that time to listen and talk with HIM,** I cannot reach the deepest level of intimacy with Him. God is always listening to me and to you and He will always answer us. You may not get the answer immediately but God will answer every one of your questions. One word from the Lord can truly change our lives and inspire us to get our priorities in order.

God is forever calling us to an intimate relationship with Him through our Lord Jesus Christ. As you read this book, may you be refreshed and blessed and grow closer to the Lord.

I am very thankful to my sister Della Hemphill and for all those who played a role in getting this book to press. I am eternally grateful for their contributions.

May God be glorified and magnified as you read this book. May we never forget the price that Jesus paid to redeem us as he was nailed to the wooden cross. Jesus paid a debt He did not owe for you and for me. God sacrificed his only begotten son. Herein lies the perfect sacrifice.

May we never forget that we are trees of righteousness planted in the house of the Lord. May we go forth rejoicing forevermore in the joy of knowing the Lord and walking with Him.

Chapter 1
Redemption

1st Corinthians 1:30 (KJV)

"But of him are ye in Christ Jesus, who of God is made unto us wisdom and righteousness and sanctification, and redemption."

We do not have to strive for wisdom, righteousness, sanctification and redemption. When we receive Christ Jesus into our hearts, God makes these gifts abound to us. They are gifts of grace. God's grace to us is immeasurable and unfathomable.

Hebrews 9:12 (KJV)

"Neither by the blood of goats and calves, but by his own blood he entered in once into the holy place, having obtained eternal redemption for us."

Every year before Jesus came in the flesh and was born of the Virgin Mary, when the Jews celebrated Passover, a spotless lamb had to be sacrificed for the remission of the sins of the people. The lamb has to be without any blemishes or spots. This ritual had to be repeated every year to take away the sins of the people. The sacrifice would only last a year. When Jesus came, He became the perfect Passover Lamb. In contrast, Jesus, The Lamb of God gave his blood sacrifice one time and gave us eternal redemption. His sacrifice took away our sins once **and for all.**

Redemption is the action of saving or being saved from sin, error, or evil. It also means the action of regaining or gaining possession of something in exchange for payment, or clearing a debt. Redeem means to buy back.

Glory be to God, for He sent his son Jesus to redeem us from sin, sickness and poverty forevermore. Praise be to God for Jesus's death, burial and resurrection.

When I was very young and asked Jesus to come into my heart, I was thrilled and amazed that Jesus loved me so much that He chose to die on the cross and that God loved us so much that He chose to give his only begotten Son for us. When I meditate on all the suffering that Jesus had to endure, it brings me to tears. Jesus carried the weight of the world upon his shoulders. No wonder we are to rejoice in the Lord at all times. We rejoice for the great things God has done through His Son, Jesus Christ.

As the years went by, I wanted to study more about this subject of redemption. I read in the Bible about Jesus going through excruciating agony in the Garden of Gethsemane. He asked His disciples to sit down while he prayed. Jesus asked his favorites, Peter, James and John to stay, watch and pray that they may not enter into temptation. Jesus prayed a short distance away.

He prayed, "Lord, if you can, please let this cup pass from me. Nevertheless, not my will but yours be done." Three times Jesus beseeched His Father God to let the cup pass from Him.

Jesus was in such distress that his sweat was like great drops of blood falling to the ground. He was preparing for his time of suffering on the cross.

The disciples had fallen asleep as Jesus was being pressed on every side. Jesus said, "Could you not tarry one hour?"

I have learned in my walk with the Lord that I, too, can pray when I am going through any type of circumstance, "Lord, not my will but thine be done."

You can read the account in Luke 22, Matthew 26 or Mark 14.

For years now, when I do not want to go through something or deal with something, I first and foremost take it to the altar, tell my Heavenly Father all about it and pray "Lord, not my will but thine be done."

Let me encourage you that no matter how bleak your circumstances may appear, you can take them straight to your Heavenly Father. God will get you through every fiery trial and you will come out smelling like a rose. Please order my book, <u>Into The Fire.</u> God is with you and you are **more** than an overcomer.

The cross upon which Jesus died shows us how God loves us with an unconditional love. Not only did Jesus have nails driven into His hands and feet, more blood would be shed as they pressed the crown of thorns into his brow and pierced his side with a sword. We do not have to earn God's love. No, we just accept His unmerited love. We receive every promise from God by faith and by God's amazing grace.

Ephesians 1:7 (KJV)

"In whom we have redemption through his blood, the forgiveness of sins, according to the riches of His grace."

Again, Christ has redeemed us according to His matchless grace. God's grace is more than amazing. We have God's riches at Christ's expense.

You can read in John 1:29-34 about a time when John the Baptist saw Jesus coming and said, "Behold the Lamb of God who takes away the sin of the world." John said that he saw the Spirit descending from heaven like a dove, and it remained upon Jesus when He was being baptized by John. John declared that Jesus was the Son of God.

Jesus bought our freedom with his sacrifice on the cross of Calvary. He shed his own blood for you and for me and has made us to be the righteousness of God in Him.

Redeemed!! Oh how I love to acknowledge that I am redeemed by the blood of the lamb. He bought me back. Jesus is the Lamb of God who takes away the sins of the world.

Luke 22:14-15 (KJV)

"And when the hour was come, he sat down, and the twelve apostles with him. And he said unto them, With desire I have desired to eat this Passover with you before I suffer."

Matthew 5:17 tells us that Jesus came to fulfill the law, not to destroy it. He first celebrated the Passover with His apostles and later he became the new Passover Lamb.

After supper, Jesus took the bread and gave thanks and he took the cup and gave thanks. Communion is a reminder that the body of Jesus Christ was broken for us and His blood was shed for us.   When we partake of communion, we are to remember His death until His second coming.

While we were being quarantined during the coronavirus, I was sitting in my sunroom in South Carolina talking on the phone with my sister. Looking up at the sky, I saw a cloud formation that looked like the Lion of the Tribe of Judah. Following behind was the most beautiful spotless lamb I have ever seen. This lamb had no blemishes or spots.   Lastly, in this production of cloud formations was someone riding on a beautiful majestic white horse.

As the pictures remained in the sky, it was as if I could reach out and gently touch the precious spotless white lamb.

Immediately, I searched the scriptures that would explain the display that I had just witnessed. I was in awe of such a cloud formation and amazed that they were now all connected in one diorama.

Jesus first came as the suffering servant. As the perfect spotless lamb, He was slain for the sins of the world and paid the price for us all there at Calvary. He will return for us one day riding a white horse as the Lion of the Tribe of Judah.

Let us begin in the beginning when Adam and Eve were in the beautiful Garden of Eden. Everything was pure and holy; there was nothing impure in the Garden of Eden. You remember the story of Eve being tempted by Satan and how she did exactly what God had commanded them not to do.

Genesis 2:16-18 (AMP)

"And the LORD God commanded the man, saying, "You may freely (unconditionally) eat [the fruit] from every tree of the garden; but [only] from the tree of the knowledge (recognition) of good and evil you shall not eat, otherwise on the day that you eat from it, you shall most certainly die [because of your disobedience].

Now the LORD God said, "It is not good (beneficial) for the man to be alone; I will make him a helper [one who balances him—a counterpart who is] suitable *and* complementary for him."

We know that they did not die physically, but they died spiritually when they disobeyed God.

God specifically said "Do not" eat from the tree of the knowledge of good and evil. Somehow, we have difficulty hearing **do not** or **don't**.

I recall one of the tours we took from our cruise ship in the Caribbean. We got off the cruise ship and rode a bus to Haiti. Snorkeling was on our agenda.   We all put on our gear and headed toward the water.

First of all, since my swimming abilities were very poor, I was very nervous. After we walked into the water, I realized that I had forgotten to take off my watch. For an excuse to get out of the water, I quickly said, "I have to go back and take off my watch."

My husband could see the fear in my face and was very cognizant of the problem I was facing. Immediately, he encouraged me to get into the snorkeling class they were having up on this little hill. I placed my watch in our belongings and then joined the class. The instructor told us to put on our life jacket. We followed her instruction. Then, she said, "Don't inflate your vest until I finish with my lesson."

Immediately, I inflated my vest because I did not hear the word "Don't." I was a little embarrassed and I was experiencing a lot of fear.

After all the instructions, she took us out into the water and told us to stand in the slightly murky water about 6 feet away from her and then swim toward her. Everyone followed her instructions except for me.

I stood frozen in the water because of my fear. She sensed my hesitance and after she dismissed the lesson, she took me to a more beautiful and pristine water place. No one was there but us and the water was a clear beautiful turquoise. It was a perfect paradise.

She held my hand while we snorkeled together. She taught me how to turn around when we stopped and let the foot fins be in front of me. It was so beautiful seeing all the fish, coral, etc. There were myriad beautiful colors under the water.

I felt like a 5 year old and I was very grateful that she was so patient, understanding, and caring. To my husband's delight, she invited him to join us in this private pristine water. We snorkeled together for a long time. As long as she held my hand, I was very happy and knew I was safe in her care.

I have not changed a bit. I am constantly aware that God is holding my right hand and will never let go. No matter what I am going through, God is with me and God will never leave me or forsake me.

Isaiah 41:13 (KJV)

"For I the Lord thy God will hold thy right hand, saying unto thee, Fear not; I will help thee."

While I was working on my Education Degree, we learned from our behavior management class that children seldom hear the word don't. So we were taught to say, "We **will do** this or that." I could totally understand. Sometimes students are so eager to please their teachers as soon as they hear instructions, they do it without realizing you said **Don't** in the beginning of the sentence.

I was so eager to please and follow the instructions of my snorkeling instructor that I did not hear the word **Don't** inflate until I noticed that no one had inflated their vest except for me.

When God had commanded them to obey him, apparently Eve did not hear the words **do not** eat of the tree of life and Adam did not heed the words do not. Nevertheless, whether they heard it or not, they still chose to disobey.

When Eve saw that the tree of the knowledge of good and evil was good for food and pretty to look at, her desire made her eat the fruit and she gave some to Adam and he ate. Eve viewed the fruit from her 5 senses and not from the eyes of God. It appears to me that what the Bible says in the following scripture is still true for us today.

1st John 2:15-16 (KJV)

"Love not the world, neither the things that are in the world. If any man loves the world, the love of the Father is not in him. For all that is in the world,

> **the lust of the flesh, and**
>
> **the lust of the eyes, and**
>
> **the pride of life,**

is not of the Father, but is of the world."

We must pay attention to what we focus on and see whether it is good, right and true. If it fits into all 3 categories, then it must be great to pursue.

After they had eaten the forbidden fruit, their eyes opened and they knew they were naked and used fig leaves to cover themselves. At this time, they heard the voice of God and they hid themselves from the presence of the Lord God among the trees in the garden.

God asked Adam to tell him where he was. Adam told him that he hid because he was afraid and he was naked.

God has all knowledge. Therefore, God knew that Adam had eaten the fruit off the tree which he was commanded not to eat. Adam tried to blame it on Eve. Then Eve blamed it on the serpent. Eve made her decision and so did Adam.

We can all make our own decisions and we cannot blame any of our decisions on someone else.

Whether we want to acknowledge it or not, we are the captain of our own ship.

We must always be cognizant of the fact that God is the Alpha and Omega. God is the beginning and the end. God knows us from our beginning to our end. God knows everything and sees everything.

Our all-knowing God wants us to tell Him the truth even though He already knows everything. It is comforting to know that God has already paved the way for us to follow Him all the days of our lives.

God has only planned good things for us. It is up to us to make the right decisions based on the fact that we have been redeemed.

Matthew 27:50-51 (KJV)

"Jesus, when he had cried again with a loud voice, yielded up the ghost. And, behold, the veil of the temple was rent in twain from the top to the bottom, and the earth did quake, and the rocks rent;"

Under the old covenant, the veil in the temple separated the Israelites from the direct presence of God. This veil was made of blue, purple, and scarlet yarn with cherubim woven in by a skilled craftsman.

The veil was hung by gold hooks on a wooden frame overlaid with gold and the Ark of the Covenant was kept behind the veil. No one other than the **high priest** was allowed to enter into the Holy of Holies, and this was only once a year with the blood of a sacrificial lamb.

Hebrews 4:16 (KJV)

"Let us therefore come boldly unto the throne of grace that we may obtain mercy, and find grace to help in time of need."

Do you need mercy? Do you need grace? Do you want help in your time of need? God and our Redeemer Jesus Christ are saying to you, "Come boldly and receive the best for you now." Take every concern and lay it down at the feet of Jesus.

When Jesus died on the cross, He opened unto us the privilege of going directly into the presence of God. Under the new covenant of His blood, we are no longer under the law but under grace. We can enter God's throne room boldly any time. We can enter NOW covered by the blood of Jesus Christ.

God gave me a picture of the veil being torn from the top to the bottom through a vision when he set me free from a fearful memory.

My husband, Rusty and I attended an Episcopal Marriage Encounter. We were trying to learn how to communicate more effectively with each other in our new marriage.

It turned out to be much more than a couple's encounter. It was also a wonderful encounter with the Lord. We did learn how to communicate well in our marriage, but the most significant thing that happened to me spiritually was that I let go of a terrible memory.

The minister sent the men to their rooms and the women stayed in the main sanctuary. After the men had left the room, they asked us to think about the most fearful event we had ever encountered. The first thing that came to my mind was the time when I was locked inside a panel van around the age of 7. A panel van does not have any windows in the back. I was outside in the parking lot of the church where my Dad and Mom pastored. In the darkness, I felt all alone. I remembered feeling the fear of being abandoned and helpless.

After the women had time to process, the ministers at the Marriage Encounter then instructed us to change places with our spouses. The men came to the sanctuary and we went to our rooms to talk to the Lord about the most fearful thing that had happened to us. As I continued to talk to the Lord, I was in so much emotional pain that I asked the Lord **not** to show me anything else about my fear until the next morning.

When I finally fell asleep, I slept well and the next morning, the husbands and wives were separated again. They sent the men to their rooms and asked the women to come to the altar and talk to the Lord again about their most fearful time. I followed the instructions and knelt at the altar.

The Lord took me back in my mind, to the place where I was locked inside the van. My Dad's friend had purchased a new delivery van for his grocery store. He stopped to get my Mom and Dad and take them for corporate prayer in the church. I jumped in the van and said that I wanted to go to church to pray with them. When we arrived, they forgot to open the door for me to get out of the van and headed on into the church.

I started screaming for help because I knew there was a friend who lived in the house next door to our church. However, no one could hear me. Later my Mom and Dad came out and found me screaming and took me back into the church to the altar and asked Jesus to heal me.

At the altar that morning in the Episcopal Marriage Encounter, I heard the Lord's voice and the Lord gave me a vision. In the vision, while I was kneeling at the altar, I saw myself inside the panel van but this time the whole van was full of light. The van doors were (torn) rent in two from top to bottom and flew open and there was Jesus, as bright as the morning star.

All fear was gone, and I was walking with the Lord as he lifted me out of the van. The light of the glorious gospel of Jesus Christ was shining so brightly that it lit up the whole town of Chesapeake. The Word of God came alive in my life that day. The Lord said, "Just like the veil was torn from top to bottom when Jesus died on the cross, today, I am tearing those van doors open from top to bottom and you are coming out and you are free."

Hebrews 9:11-12 (KJV)

"But Christ being come an high priest of good things to come, by a greater and more perfect tabernacle, not made with hands, that is to say, not of this building: Neither by the blood of goat and calves, but by his own blood he entered in once in the holy place, having obtained eternal redemption for us."

When Jesus died on the cross, He declared "It is finished" and the veil was rent (torn) from top to bottom. And once and for all we were able to go into the throne room and talk with our Father God by the blood of Jesus.

The victory that Jesus wrought for us is an eternal gift to each one of us

Now, we can come into the King's chambers and worship at His throne. God is seated on the throne and Jesus is seated at his right hand. We are seated with Christ in the heavenly places spiritually, not physically.

1 Corinthians 15:57 (KJV)

"But thanks be to God, which giveth us the victory through our Lord Jesus Christ."

1 John 5:4 (KJV)

"For whatsoever is born of God overcometh the world; and this is the victory that overcometh the world, even our faith."

We go to God in the name of Jesus and He says, "Come in." Our redemption paid for our right to go into the throne room boldly and with faith in God and not with fear. Through faith in God, we walk in His victory.

Genesis 3:24 (AMP)

"So God drove the man out; and at the east of the Garden of Eden He [permanently] stationed the cherubim and the sword with the flashing blade which turned round and round [in every direction] to protect *and* guard the way (entrance, access) to the tree of life."

What a dreadful day for the kingdom of God when Adam and Eve were not allowed to be near the tree of life. Now, God and Jesus have made a way for us to partake of Jesus, the tree of life.

Revelation 2:7 (AMP)

"He who has an ear, let him hear *and* heed what the Spirit says to the churches. To him who overcomes [the world through believing that Jesus is the Son of God], I will grant [the privilege] to eat [the fruit] from the tree of life, which is in the Paradise of God."

The good news is that Jesus came to earth to save us from our sins and defeat Satan. Because Adam sinned, we are all born into sin and we need a Savior. We need our redeemer, Jesus Christ, to save us from our sins.

Jesus redeemed us; He paid the price to guarantee us salvation, healing and deliverance. Let us think a moment about what it will be like when we all get to heaven because we have been redeemed.

Revelation 22:1-5 (AMP)

"Then the angel showed me a river of the water of life, clear as crystal, flowing from the throne of God and of the Lamb (Christ), [2] in the middle of its street. On either side of the river was the tree of life, bearing twelve *kinds of* fruit, yielding its fruit every month; and the leaves of the tree were for the healing of the nations. [3] There will no longer exist anything that is cursed [because sin and illness and death are gone]; and the throne of God and of the Lamb will be in it, and His bond-servants will serve *and* worship Him [with great awe and joy and loving devotion]; [4] they will [be privileged to] see His face, and His name will be on their foreheads. [5] And there will no longer be night; they have no need for lamplight or sunlight, because the Lord God will illumine them; and they will reign [as kings] forever and ever."

Even though Adam sinned and brought us out of the beautiful Garden of Eden and into darkness, God has delivered us out of the power of darkness into His marvelous light by the work of Christ at Calvary. We can partake of all the blessings that God has just for us when we receive Jesus into our hearts. Hallelujah!

Romans 5:17 (AMP)

"For if by the trespass of the one (Adam), death reigned through the one (Adam), much more *surely* will those who receive the abundance of grace and the free gift of righteousness reign in [eternal] life through the One, Jesus Christ."

Yes, by Adam's trespass, death reigned, but God's grace has given us the free gift of righteousness and we are to reign as kings in this life through our Lord Jesus. Our authority is in the name of Jesus.

I declare that I can do all things through Christ. The precious name of Jesus allows us to live a victorious life.

As the Holy Spirit wills, I will function in the gift of a psalmist. When I was striving to earn my way to God, but without being aware of what I was doing, I received this song:

"Jesus has done it; think not there's anything you can do. He's won the victory and He's given it straight to you. I receive it. He's given it straight to you."

Now, I have given up all striving to make things happen on my own. Now, I know that Jesus has completed everything and conquered and defeated every foe we could have in our lives, including Satan.

I was doing everything I could including teaching Sunday School, being a worship leader, being a prayer warrior for my church and teaching a Woman's Bible Study in order to gain an audience with the Most High God. I had a zeal for God, without realizing that Jesus had already paid every price for me to go into the Holy of Holies and approach God without fear and trembling.

Unfortunately, I was working toward earning my way to God. I had a passion to please God. One day a prophet came into town and said that God had put that apparent insatiable desire in me and I was elated and comforted to know it was God's work in me.

After the Lord showed me through that song that Jesus has already completed everything, my job was to receive all that Jesus had accomplished through redeeming me. I needed to rest in and have peace in the knowledge that Jesus paid it all. When Jesus died on the cross, He said, "It is finished."

After Jesus was resurrected, and returned to the right hand of the Father, he accomplished all we would ever need to live successfully in this life. In Christ, we live and move and have our being.

By the time I quit striving, I was completely worn out and went through many years of being sick. Nevertheless, I chose to keep my eyes on Jesus. My desire to know the Lord increases more and more each day. To know the Lord is to love the Lord. I can take his yoke upon me for it is easy and light.

I no longer believe that I have to earn my way in order to be pleasing to the Lord. I know as I am trusting in the Lord at all times, He is well- pleased with me. I rest now in His love, mercy and peace knowing how much God loves me. God loves you, my friend and you have been redeemed by the blood of the Lamb.

Hebrews 9:22, 24, 28 (NKJV)

"And according to the law almost all things are [a]purified with blood, and without shedding of blood there is no [b]remission."

"For Christ has not entered the holy places made with hands, *;which are* copies of the true, but into heaven itself, now to appear in the presence of God for us;"

"so Christ was offered once to bear the sins of many. To those

who eagerly wait for Him He will appear a second time, apart from sin, for salvation."

God required a blood sacrifice to cleanse our souls from sin. Every year the people had to sacrifice a pure, spotless Lamb and this sacrifice for sins only lasted one year. When Jesus sacrificed himself, He did it once and for all. Hallelujah!

Repentance is to feel or express sincere regret about one's wrongdoing or sin. True repentance is when we stop and sin no more in whatever area of difficulty that we are experiencing.

Through the work of Christ, forgiveness is always a present help; I mean always. However, it is our job to repent (to stop sinning). When we repent, we turn completely away from the wrongdoing and go forward in a godly manner. John the Baptist was sent as a forerunner to the work of Jesus Christ. John's message was repentance:

Matthew 3:1-3 (KJV)

"In those days came John the Baptist, preaching in the wilderness of Judea, And saying,

Repent ye for the kingdom of heaven is at hand.

For this is he that was spoken of by the prophet Esaias, saying, the voice of one crying in the wilderness, Prepare ye the way of the Lord, make his paths straight."

When we know the story of redemption, it is to draw us near to the heart of God so we can repent of our sins and ask Jesus to come into our hearts.

The next step is to follow Jesus in water baptism. John the Baptist had the honor of baptizing our Lord Jesus Christ. Although John was very humbled to baptize Jesus, Jesus encouraged John to do it anyway. This is what happened when Jesus was baptized.

Matthew 3:16-17 (KJV)

"And Jesus, when he was baptized, went up straightway out of the water: and, lo, the heavens were opened unto him, and he saw the Spirit of God descending like a dove, and lighting upon him: And lo a voice from heaven, saying, this is my beloved Son, in whom I am well pleased."

Sometimes, I picture God smiling on us when we do what is pleasing to Him. I know that the angels in heaven rejoice when a person comes to Christ.

Also, I believe that God is well pleased when we follow the next step of water baptism, to show that our sins are buried in the depths of the sea and we rise up as new creatures in Christ. Jesus died on the cross, was buried for 3 days and was resurrected from the grave. Baptism symbolizes the death, burial and resurrection of Jesus Christ.

Galatians 3:13-14 (AMP)

"Christ purchased our freedom *and* redeemed us from the curse of the Law *and* its condemnation by becoming a curse for us—for it is written, "CURSED IS EVERYONE WHO HANGS [crucified] ON A TREE (cross)"— in order that in Christ Jesus the blessing of Abraham might also come to the Gentiles, so that we would all receive [the realization of] the promise of the [Holy] Spirit through faith."

When Christ died on the cross, he became a curse for us so that we would be redeemed from the curse of the law. Before Jesus was crucified, buried and resurrected, man lived under the law. They were under so many curses if they did not follow the law. It is sad to read about the curses in **Deuteronomy Chapter 28**. However, it makes me happy to read about the blessings of being a child of God in this same chapter. I will tell you some of the blessings if we listen diligently to God's voice and obey God's commandments:

We will be blessed in the city.

We will be blessed in the field.

We will be blessed in the fruit of our bodies.

We will be blessed when we go in and when we come out.

The Lord will cause our enemies who rise up against us to be defeated.

The Lord will command His blessing in our storehouse.

The Lord will make His people holy to Himself.

All the people of the earth will call us blessed.

The Lord will make us have a surplus of prosperity.

The Lord will open His good treasure to us, the heavens to give us rain.

The Lord will bless whatever we put our hands to.

The Lord will make us the head and not the tail.

My heart longs to obey the Lord and follow hard after him. I have set my face like a flint to follow the Lord and obey His commandments all the days of my life.

I pray that you will join me in surrendering your will for God's perfect plan for your life. God has given us a free will and we get to choose whom we serve. As for me and my house, we choose to serve the Lord.

Jesus redeemed us from **every** curse, specifically the curse of poverty, sickness and spiritual death. For poverty, God has given us prosperity. For sickness and disease, God has given us divine health. For spiritual death, God has given us eternal life.

Poverty and lack is a curse.

Sickness and disease is a curse.

Spiritual death is a curse.

Remember, Jesus became a curse for us that we would not be under the curse anymore. Jesus does not want us to be poor, sick or spiritually without the life of God.

We give God praise, glory and honor for the redemption acquired through His precious Son, Jesus. We are forever grateful.

Our redemption is an eternal fact. Glory be to Jesus, let the Hallelujahs go up before the throne of God today.

A New Song of Praise to

My Redeemer

By Betty Kemper

My Precious Redeemer, my Savior, my friend.

How can I thank you for all you have been?

You gave your precious life on Calvary's tree

And, all because of your great love for me.

Jesus, you were the perfect sacrifice, well pleasing to God.

Now, I choose to follow your footsteps wherever you trod.

You paved the way for me to go boldly to the throne of God

Where you sit at his right hand forevermore.

I am so grateful to YOU Lord.

I thank you my Savior.

I will love you all the days of my life.

My Precious Redeemer

My Precious Redeemer

My Savior, my friend.

Chapter 2
Reconciliation

Reconciliation is the restoration of friendly relations. Restoration is the action of returning something to a former owner, place, or condition. The revelation of God always brings restoration

After the fall of Adam, man had to be reconciled to God. God, through sending his only begotten Son, made the way for us to be reconciled to Him.

2nd Corinthians 5:18-21(KJV)

"And all things are of God, who hath reconciled us to himself by Jesus Christ, and hath given to us the ministry of reconciliation; To wit, that God was in Christ, reconciling the world unto himself not imputing their trespasses unto them; and hath committed unto us the word of reconciliation.   Now then we are ambassadors for Christ, as though God did beseech you by us: we pray you in Christ's stead, be ye reconciled to God. For He hath made Him to be sin for us, who knew no sin; that we might be made the righteousness of God in him."

When a relationship has been damaged in some way, there needs to be reconciliation and restoration. We are to tell others that God loves them and God is for them and not against them. God only has good plans for them. It brings reconciliation between God and man when they know the truth about the goodness of God.

Romans 5:10 (KJV)

"For if, when we were enemies, we were reconciled to God by the death of his Son, much more, being reconciled, we shall be saved by his life."

Jesus died, was buried, and on the third day after his burial, He was resurrected from the dead. Jesus is alive forevermore.

When we become born again, we become a new creature in Christ and all things are become new. Becoming is a process.

When a man and a woman join together in holy matrimony, the

minister says, "And they shall become one." A man and a woman who have totally different backgrounds and upbringings joined together in marriage. My husband and I have been married for 41 years and we are still becoming one. I can say that it is far better than in the beginning but we still strive to   improve our union, especially in the areas of effective communication and walking in unity. A house divided against itself cannot stand.

When we become a new creature, we learn the ways of the Lord line upon line and precept upon precept. We renew our minds as we study the bible and spend time in prayer. Spiritually, we become a new creation immediately. However, it takes time to become new in our minds and get rid of a lot of stinking thinking.

Jesus died on the tree. The cross where Jesus died is a shelter for us. I can still remember as a child visualizing the cross and laying all my burdens down at the foot. I still do that to this very day.

I love to go to the altar in the front of the church when I am carrying burdens that I am not meant to carry. By the way, we are not meant to carry any burdens.   I lay those burdens down at Jesus' feet and leave them there at the altar. Laying my burdens down at the altar gives me a place of reference. When that burden tries to come back on me, I declare, "I put that on the altar!

One day when I was preaching, the Lord told me to encourage the people to go to the altar if they had any need and give it to Jesus. During the next meeting, a man testified that his back was healed when he took the problem to Jesus at the altar that night. Glory be to God!

Jesus knew no sin and yet he became sin for us. Maybe you are not called to be an ordained minister, but we are all called to be ministers of reconciliation.

Colossians 1:20 (KJV)

"And, having made peace through the blood of his cross, by him to reconcile all things unto himself; by him, I say, whether they be things in earth, or things in heaven."

If anyone comes to you and asks you how to pray for someone to reconcile to another person, please give them this scripture. I have prayed this prayer for many people and they have told me of their success. The Word works.

This is my prayer:

Heavenly Father, I thank you for making peace through the blood of your cross to reconcile all things unto yourself. Now I lift up ___________ and ___________ to you. Father, please reconcile them both to you first and then to each other. Father, I pray for complete restoration in their relationship. In Jesus's name, Amen.

Picture a triangle with Jesus at the top and one person on the bottom left of the triangle and the other person on the bottom right side. Now, as each person goes up the triangle to Jesus, they end up in the lap of the Lord together in His presence. The blood of Jesus is enough to reconcile people to God and to each other. Hallelujah

How many times have we tried to do what is good, right, and true and tried to be the best we can be? Once we realize that we are the righteousness of God in Christ Jesus, we will no longer allow condemnation to attack us. There is no condemnation to those who are in Christ Jesus.

Isaiah 61:1a, 3 (AMP)

V. 1 "The Spirit of the Lord GOD is upon me, Because the LORD has anointed *and* commissioned me to bring good news ..."

V. 3 "To grant to those who mourn in Zion *the following*: To give them a [c]turban instead of dust [on their heads, a sign of mourning], the oil of joy instead of mourning, the garment [expressive] of praise instead of a disheartened spirit. So they will be called the trees of righteousness [strong and magnificent, distinguished for integrity, justice, and right standing

with God], the planting of the LORD, that He may be glorified."

As "Ready Reconcilers" (ministers of reconciliation), we are to bring the good news, not the bad news. We are all made in the image and likeness of God. As believers, we have been made the righteousness of God in Christ Jesus. How do we respond to this great gift of grace from God? As someone who is a minister of reconciliation, we can ask ourselves these questions:

Do we comfort all those who mourn?

Do we give the oil of joy to those who mourn in Zion?

Do we encourage them to put on the garment of praise for the spirit of heaviness?

Do we share the good news that our Heavenly Father welcomes us any time day or night, and we can go boldly into the throne room and ask for grace to help in times of trouble?

God has given us the key to an abundant life and he has given us the authority to rule and reign in our lives. He gave us our own will and the ability to make our own choices.

God is always a present help in the times of trouble. I have learned to run to Him, and say No to everything else that does not line up with the word of God.

Jesus is a storehouse of wisdom to me and a tower of strength. Jesus is our tree of life.   We must always remember that our battle is not against flesh and blood but against wickedness in high places--in other words, the devil and his cohorts.

We have the treasure of Christ in us, our hope of glory. Christ is in our earthen vessel by the power of the Holy Spirit. Selah! The power that works in us is from God and not from ourselves. We cannot earn or work up this power.

2nd Corinthians 4:6-11

"For God, who commanded the light to shine out of darkness, hath shined in our hearts, to give the light of the knowledge of the glory of God in the face of Jesus Christ. But we have this treasure in earthen vessels, that the Excellency of the power may be of God, and not of us. We are troubled on every side, yet not distressed; we are perplexed, but not in despair; Persecuted, but not forsaken; cast down, but not destroyed; always bearing about in the body the dying of the Lord

Jesus, that the life also of Jesus might be made manifest in our body. For we which live are always delivered unto death for Jesus' sake, that the life also of Jesus might be made manifest in our mortal flesh."

Sometimes we go through trouble on every side, yet we face it without becoming distressed. Sometimes we are confused, but we do not fall into despair. Even when we are persecuted by people, God does not forsake us.

We know that God raised Jesus from the dead and He will also raise us up through Jesus. Paul said that in his ministry, he suffered for our sakes, so that God's grace through the thanksgiving of us and others may overflow to the glory of God.

Paul says that our little battles are working an eternal weight of glory.

We have been reconciled to God by Jesus Christ. We are partakers of His divine nature and we walk in love because God is love. The Bible says in:

James 3:11 (KJV)

"Doth a fountain send forth at the same place sweet water and bitter?"

We need to examine our hearts periodically because if we have bitterness and envy in us, we need to go back to the cross. We can be a ready reconciler as we keep our hearts and minds pure and full of love. God is total love and expects us to walk in total love. When evil speaking spews out of our mouths, it is ungodly. Do we lay Jesus aside while we have our outrages of anger toward others? Do we lay Jesus aside while we criticize and condemn others?

When a person is born again, his mind is not instantly changed. He is changed as he renews his mind by studying the Word of God. When you get saved, your spirit comes alive, but your mind has a lot of work to do to line up with the Lord, who now lives in you.

When an acorn sprouts, most of its energy is spent on root development. There is little growth above ground. Branch growth begins and then the taproot is given into a big root system.

When we are born again, it is the beginning of growing our roots in Christ. Immediately, we become the righteousness of God in Christ. However, it takes studying the Bible, praying, and spending time with the Lord to renew your mind.

We become a new creation when we are born again. However, it takes time to grow into that huge oak of righteousness. Renewing our minds is a process.

You will know a Christian, first of all by the love they show. The only thing that has any profit is when it is done in love. Anything we do profits us nothing without love. You can do magnificent things, perform magnificent tasks, but without love it is nothing. A heart of love produces caring understanding, gentleness, kindness and a caring spirit.

We are to guard our hearts with all diligence. A heart of hate produces jealousy, envying and strife. The Bible says in **James 3:16**, where there is strife, there is every evil work. It is imperative that we strive for unity in our families and in our churches.

To produce good fruit, we must abide in the vine. A tree grows from a strong root system. Jesus is the vine and we are the branches. The only way we can produce good fruit is to abide in Jesus, the vine.

John 15:5 (KJV)

"I am the vine, ye are the branches: He that abideth in me, and I in him, the same bringeth forth much fruit: for without me ye can do nothing."

When we walk in the Spirit, we do not fulfill the lusts of the flesh. It started with Eve in the garden when she saw the tree was good with her eyes. She obeyed the lusts of her flesh instead of the instructions from her Father God.

When Jesus went back to the Father, he sent us His Holy Spirit. We are the righteousness of God in Christ

Jesus; we have the Holy Spirit to teach, guide and direct us. Jesus has been made to us wisdom, so we have the wisdom we need to make good decisions.

When we know that we need more wisdom, we just ask God for more wisdom and He will give more wisdom to us. When we have a check in our Spirit, that is a NO, do not do that. May we daily obey the voice of the Lord and follow through when he is directing/instructing us in righteousness.

We can pray that the love of God can be perfected in us. I have met a few people and the love of God just oozes out of them. They have no agenda except to allow the love of God that is shed abroad in their hearts to flow out to others.

A tree is known by the fruit it produces. A Christian is known by the fruit he/she produces.

Galatians 6:7-10 (KJV)

"Be not deceived; God is not mocked; for whatsoever a man soweth, that shall he also reap. For he that soweth to his flesh shall of the flesh reap corruption; but he that soweth to the Spirit shall of the Spirit reap life everlasting. And let us not be weary in well doing; for in due season we shall reap, if we faint not. As we have therefore opportunity, let us do good unto all men especially unto them who are of the household of faith."

An orange tree produces only oranges. An apple tree produces only apples. As a Christian we are only to produce the fruit of the Spirit which is:

Love

Joy

Peace

Longsuffering

Gentleness

Goodness

Faith

Meekness

Temperance

See **Galatians 5:22.**

We are like a tree in the house of God. The above is the fruit of the Spirit which lives in us. We must examine our hearts whenever anything contrary to the fruit of the Spirit comes out of our hearts and then out of our mouths.

We are to stir up the gifts of God in us; the fruit of the Spirit of God. We can stir up these gifts in us because they already abide in us. When I need more love, I stir up the fruit of love in me by the power of the Holy Spirit. When I need more joy, I stir up that gift within me. The fruit of the Spirit is in me. The Holy Spirit produces good fruit in me at all times.

God really cares about our conversations and he wants us to have a pure conversation with anyone we come in contact with in this world. God looks for a pure heart that He can bless even more.

Let us pray:

Heavenly Father,

Thank you so much for sending your son Jesus to reconcile us back to you. Father, today help us to become the ministers of reconciliation that you have called us to be. We go forth not by might, nor by power, but by the Holy Spirit. We receive the call to be a minister of reconciliation to the world. In Jesus name. Amen.

Chapter 3
Righteousness

Proverbs 12:28 (KJV)

"In the way of righteousness is life; and in the pathway thereof there is no death."

Every day as we acknowledge that we are the righteousness of God in Christ Jesus, we draw closer to the Lord. When we choose righteousness, we choose life. God is life, light and love.

Jesus is the tree of life. Jesus paid the full price. Jesus has been made unto us wisdom, **righteousness** and sanctification. Righteousness is the quality or state of being just or rightful.

As born-again believers, we are to do the following:

Ephesians 4:22-32 (KJV)

"That ye put off concerning the former conversation the old man, which is corrupt according to the deceitful lusts; and be renewed in the spirit of your mind;

And that ye put on the new man, which after God is created in righteousness and true holiness.

Wherefore putting away all lying, speak every man truth with his neighbour; for we are members one of another. Be ye angry, and sin not; let not the sun go down upon your wrath:

Neither give place to the devil. Let him that stole steal no more; but

rather let him labour, working with his hands the thing which is good, that he may have to give to him that needeth.

Let no corrupt communication proceed out of your mouth, but that which is good to the use of edifying, that it may minister grace unto the hearers.

And grieve not the Holy Spirit of God, whereby ye are sealed unto the day of redemption.

Let all bitterness, and wrath, and anger, and clamour, and evil speaking, be put away from you, with all malice: And be ye kind one to another, tenderhearted, forgiving one another, even as God for Christ's sake hath forgiven you."

Ephesians is clear about what our actions need to be. The Bible says that, as born-again believers we are to let our light shine so all the world can see the reflection of Christ in us.

2nd Corinthians 3:18 (KJV)

"But we all, with open face beholding as in a glass the glory of the Lord, are changed into the same image from glory to glory, even as by the Spirit of the Lord."

We do not work to earn the right to become the righteousness of God in Christ Jesus. The Bible says that we are the righteousness of God in Christ Jesus. Becoming the righteousness of God in Christ Jesus is who we are because of our day of salvation. It is the day we invited Jesus to come into our hearts.

Because God sent his son, Jesus to us, we are made the **righteousness** of God in Christ Jesus the moment we receive Christ into our hearts. Knowing our redemption and knowing we are the righteousness of God in Christ causes us to rejoice.

God loved us so much that he sent his only begotten Son to die on the cross for us. Jesus was the once and for all holy sacrifice to cleanse us from all of our sins. He came to deliver us out of darkness into his marvelous light. Jesus is light, love and life.

Isaiah 61:3 (KJV)

"To appoint unto them that mourn in Zion, to give unto them beauty for ashes, the oil of joy for mourning, the garment of praise for the spirit of heaviness; that they might be called trees of righteousness, the planting of the Lord, that He might be glorified."

In Psalm 52:8, we also find that we are like a green olive tree in the house of the Lord. We are trees of righteousness because all of the work that Jesus did at Calvary. Christ, our hope of glory, lives within us.

Do we realize that **Isaiah 61:3 (NIV)** calls us **"oaks of righteousness, a planting of the Lord for the display of his splendor?"**

Do we realize that like a tree, (Jesus the tree of life), we are strong, magnificent, distinguished for uprightness, justice, and right standing with God, the creator of heaven and earth?

1st Peter 2:22-24 (KJV)

"Who did no sin, neither was guile found in his mouth: Who, when he was reviled, reviled not again; when he suffered, he threatened not; but committed himself to him that judgeth righteously: Who his own self bare our sins in his own body on the tree, that we, being dead to sins,

should live unto righteousness: by whose stripes ye were healed."

Before we go any further, let us take a look at the magnificent oak trees that God made in the beginning when God created the heavens and our planet Earth.

Naturally, I am not an oak tree, but I have been stripped of my leaves many times from harsh words spoken to me. I have felt forsaken and cast down. However, since my root system is in Jesus, I have always survived the ferocious attacks on my spirit, my soul and my body.

2 Corinthians 4:16-18(KJV)

"For which cause we faint not; but though our outward man perishes, yet the inward man is renewed day by day. For our light affliction, which is but for a moment, worketh for us a far more exceeding and

eternal weight of glory; While we look not at the things which are seen, but at the things which are not seen; for the things which are seen are temporal; but the things which are not seen are eternal."

Our trials and afflictions are temporary. God is holding our hand in each trial and God only wants good for us. God is good and he does good all the time. We rejoice in the fact that God is on our side and if God is for us nobody can be against us.

The oak tree is one of the most loved trees and is a symbol of strength, morale, resistance and knowledge. It is considered a storehouse of wisdom and a tower of strength.

The bark of the oak has been said to have medicinal qualities. We know that having a merry heart is like having good medicine. Laugh a lot. Laugh on purpose.

Jesus is the tree of life. Jesus paid the full price. Jesus has been made unto us wisdom, righteousness and sanctification.

The oak tree can withstand terrible hurricanes and tornadoes. Likewise, living in Florida has given us the opportunity to withstand many harsh storms. God has delivered us out of them all. Even when oak trees are stripped of their leaves, they survive because of their strength. The joy of the Lord is our strength. The oak trees have curvy branches and a strong root system. Our root system is in the rock, Jesus Christ.

Some oak trees grow more than 100 feet high and can live over 300 years. God also promises us longevity. God says in the following scripture:

Psalm 91:16 (AMP)

"With long life I will satisfy him and I will let him see My salvation."

Oak trees are a great source of shade. Psalm 91 tells us he that dwelleth in the secret place of the Most High shall abide under the **shadow** of the Almighty.

We are to live unto righteousness. Every day, we can choose to awake to righteousness for God has made the way. God's grace is sufficient.

1st Corinthians 15:34a (KJV)

"Awake to righteousness…,"

When we truly grasp that we are the righteousness of God in Christ, sin will be kicked out every time it knocks on our door. Jesus became sin, so we would never have to choose sin. We can always choose to walk in what is good, right and true. Let us truly awake to righteousness!

Remember that Abraham believed in the Lord and it was counted to him for righteousness. When we believe in the Lord, it is counted to us for righteousness. Only believe. All things are possible if we only believe.

Dear Heavenly Father,

Thank you so much for your gift of righteousness. It did not cost us anything, but it cost Jesus his life.

We praise you Father, Son and Holy Spirit. May your kingdom be established in us today. May we truly be the oaks of righteousness that you have called us to be.

Father, teach us more in depth concerning our righteousness in you in

Christ Jesus. Father, we are hungry for you and we thank you for putting that desire in us to follow you with all our heart, soul and strength.

Father, we are saturated with your love, with your peace, with your joy and with everything that is right, good and true by the power of the Holy Spirit in Jesus name, Amen.

Chapter 4
Rejoicing

Rejoicing is the action of a person who rejoices. To rejoice is to feel joyful and to be delighted.

1 Chronicles 16:31 (KJV)

"Let the heavens be glad, and let the earth rejoice; and let men say among the nations, "The Lord reigneth."

When I think of the word rejoice, I immediately think of the wise men looking for the star so they could find the Christ child. When they finally saw the star, they **rejoiced** with great joy. See **Matthew 2:10.** When they came into the house, they worshipped him and opened their presents of gold, frankincense and myrrh.

In order to rejoice, we must first experience joy in our heart, mind and soul. Can you think of a time when you lost something? When you finally found it, your heart was filled with joy.

My favorite verse that the Lord gave me in a song concerning rejoicing is found in:

Zechariah 2:10 (KJV)

"Sing and rejoice Oh Daughter of Zion. Sing and rejoice Oh Daughter of Zion, for lo I come and I will dwell in the midst of thee, saith the Lord."

Nehemiah 8:10 tells us that the joy of the Lord is our strength. When we have the joy of the Lord down in our hearts, it will manifest through our mouths and our actions with thanksgiving.

I think of it this way. When we have joy in our hearts, we can rejoice again and again, with joy unspeakable.

Circumstances, people and the enemy will try to steal your joy. May the joy of the Lord abound in your heart. The more you rejoice, the more you will want to rejoice. To me, rejoice means to have joy over and over again.

Ecclesiastes 3:1 (AMP)

"There is a season (a time appointed) for everything and a time for every delight and event or purpose under heaven."

There is a time to rejoice and be glad. When someone is in mourning, it is time for us to help bear their burdens to the Lord. We can pray for them and have compassion.

Why in the world would we want to rejoice in the Lord always? Why are we to give thanks in everything? It is very simple. We are to rejoice in the Lord always because He saved us and delivered out of a life of bondage into His glorious kingdom which is righteousness, peace and joy in the Holy Ghost, according to **1st Peter 2:9.**

We do not thank God that something bad happened to us, but we thank Him that He works all things out for our good. We can rejoice in all things because we have faith in God to **bring us through** every problem.

When I had a bicycle accident, I did not feel like rejoicing. However, I made a decision to thank the Lord that I was still alive. I rejoiced that His love was toward me and that He was healing me even though I was still in pain. I trusted God that His word was true and that He was touched with the feelings of my infirmities. I walked by faith and not by sight. I rejoiced for many reasons and I will share some of them with you:

*Jesus **saved my soul** when I was sinking deep in sin. I was very young when I asked Jesus to come into my heart. God has forgiven me of all my sins and the blood of Jesus is enough to save me and deliver me from all unrighteousness.

*I love the fact that God has given us everything that pertains to life and godliness.

*I love the fact that according to the following scripture, we are seated with Christ in the heavenly places.

Ephesians 2: 4-8 (KJV)
"But God, who is rich in mercy, for his great love wherewith he loved us, Even when we were dead in sins hath quickened us together with Christ (by grace are ye saved) And hath raised us up together and made us sit together in heavenly places in Christ Jesus. That in the ages to come he might shew the exceeding riches of his grace in his kindness toward us through Christ Jesus. For by grace are you saved through faith; and that not of yourselves; it is the gift of God."

I love to rejoice and praise God for his protection, guidance, and for never leaving me alone.

According to:

Ephesians 2:10 (KJV)

"We are his workmanship, created in Christ Jesus unto good works, which God hath before ordained that we should walk in them."

*God created us in His own image and likeness and ordained us to walk in good works; that is amazing.

*I rejoice that I am a daughter of the Most High God.

*Yes, I love to rejoice because God gave me the gift of the Holy Spirit with the evidence of speaking in tongues. When I do not know how to pray, the Holy Spirit prays through me the perfect prayer to God.

*I am forever grateful and that is a cause to rejoice. If I had a thousand tongues, it would not be sufficient to thank Him and rejoice in all He has accomplished for me.

*When I keep my mind stayed upon the Lord, I have perfect peace or Shalom.

*God's mercies are new every morning, so I can rejoice.

*God gives me life and breath; that is a cause to rejoice.

*God knows what I need even before I ask. He is all-knowing and cares about our smallest needs.

According to the Bible, God has reserved a victor's crown and he will give us our award on that great day of the Lord. Let us read:

II Timothy 4:8 (AMP)

"In the future there is reserved for me the [victor's] crown of righteousness [for being right with God and doing right], which the Lord, the righteous Judge, will award to me on that [great] day— and not to me only, but also to all those who have loved *and* longed for *and* welcomed His appearing."

When we receive our victor's crown, I believe we will lay them down at the feet of Jesus. We are to yearn for the second return of Christ and I do. I was thinking about the greatest reason for me to rejoice and I think it is the fact that we are seated with Christ in the heavenly places, and we will never die spiritually. We will live in heaven with God forever and ever throughout eternity. We will partake of the Marriage Supper of the Lamb. What a day of rejoicing that will be when we meet our Savior face to face.

Jesus was the greatest teacher there will ever be. He taught in parables. I love to read the parables listed in Luke 15 in the Amplified version.

Jesus taught how the shepherd would leave the 99 sheep to look for a lost one and rejoice when it was found. He also taught about a woman having 10 silver drachmas. If she loses one coin, she lights a lamp and searches for it until it is found and then she and everyone rejoices.

I will paraphrase my favorite parable that Jesus, the master teacher, taught in **Luke 15 (AMP).**

A man had two sons. Basically, there was a wise son and a foolish son. The younger son decided he wanted his inheritance and was bold enough to ask his father to give him his portion.

His father gave him his inheritance and very soon afterward, the younger son decided to leave home. He wasted his entire inheritance without thinking about any consequences.

Worse than being broke, there also came a famine upon that country. When he sought a job, he was sent into the fields to feed the hogs. He started thinking clearly and realized that he needed to go back home and ask his father for forgiveness.

He forthwith started the journey to see his father and return home. While he was still far away from home, his Father saw him and was moved with pity. He ran to meet his son who immediately repented to his father.

The father was ecstatic; his heart was filled with joy that his son who was lost was now found. The father brought out a robe of honor and put it on him. He gave him a ring for his hand and sandals for his feet. He had his servants kill a fattened calf and had a feast.

On the other hand, the older son who had been in the field approached the house, where he could hear music and dancing. When he was told that there was rejoicing since his younger brother had come home, the elder son became very angry and felt slighted. "What about me?" I could hear him say to his Father.

Luke 15:29-30 (AMP)

"But he said to his father, 'Look! These many years I have served you, and I have never neglected *or*

disobeyed your command. Yet you have never given me [so much as] a young goat, so that I might celebrate with my friends; ³⁰but when this [other] son of yours arrived, who has devoured your estate with immoral women, you slaughtered that fattened calf for him!"

The father told his elder son that everything belonged to him, so why would he be upset.

His father reassured him that having a feast and rejoicing was all in proper order because his younger brother was dead but is alive again. He was lost and is now found.

I want to assure you that no matter what you have done or how much of your life you have wasted, God is still looking for you to come to Him.

Luke 15:10 (AMP)

"In the same way, I tell you, there is joy in the presence of the angels of God over one sinner who repents [that is, changes his inner self—his old way of thinking, regrets past sins, lives his life in a way that proves repentance; and seeks God's purpose for his life."]

When anyone comes to Jesus and becomes born again, the angels of God **rejoice**. Everyone is equally important to God and God is joyfully excited when you come home to Jesus.

Isaiah 55:12 (KJV)

"For ye shall go out with joy, and be led forth with peace; the mountains and the hills shall break forth before you into singing, and all the trees of the field shall clap their hands."

As a native of West Virginia, every time I go back to visit, I think of this scripture and I visualize the mountains and the hills singing and all the trees on the mountains and the hills clapping their hands. I rejoice that I am alive and filled with the joy of the Lord. I sing this scripture over and over again as I travel the journey back to the place where I was born.

Isaiah 51:11 (KJV)

"Therefore the redeemed of the Lord shall return, and come with singing unto Zion; and everlasting joy shall be upon their head; they shall obtain gladness and joy, and sorrow and mourning shall flee away."

Again, we rejoice because we have been redeemed. We have been made the righteousness of God in Christ Jesus. Sometimes, we go through trials and tribulations and the sorrow and mourning can be great, but

God said that everlasting joy is on our heads.

Revelation 22:11-14 (KJV)

"He that is unjust, let him be unjust still; and he which is filthy, let him be filthy still; and he that is righteous, let him be righteous still; and he that is holy, let him be holy still. And, behold, I come quickly; and my reward is with me, to give every man according as his work shall be.

I am Alpha and Omega, the beginning and the end, the first and the last.

Blessed are they that do his commandments, that they may have right to the tree of life, and may enter in through the gates into the city."

We can truly rejoice because our name has been written in the Lamb's Book of Life. Hallelujah!!! There is a highway to heaven and the pure in heart shall see the Lord.

Let us pray:

Dear Heavenly Father, we thank you and praise you for the perfect work at Calvary.

We are eternally grateful that Jesus once and for all paid the price for our sins and removed our sins from us as far as the east is from the west.

Abba Father, may we always hear your voice and obey you as we rise each morning. When we are privileged to hear your voice, it fills us with joy unspeakable.

We decree and declare that we take that joy you have so graciously given to us and walk in obedience to your word. We go forth today in great joy that we have been redeemed. God you are magnificent and holy.

We just want to rejoice in you all the time. When we rejoice in you, our hearts are filled with peace, love, and joy. We choose to keep our minds on you because we trust you Father.

Father, we adore you in Jesus name Amen

It means to restore or maintain by renewing supply, to replenish, to stimulate and to update or renew.

Renew implies a restoration of what had become faded or disintegrated so that it seems like new. Restore implies a return to an original state after loss. If you are unsure of whether the content you are viewing on your computer is up to date, you can touch refresh and have the latest information.

Our Heavenly Father wants us to be revived and He will revive us when we spend time with Him in Bible Study, and in His presence. In His presence is the greatest refreshing one can ever gain. God is our source of supply in every area of our lives.

Leviticus 25:4-5 (KJV)

"But in the seventh year shall be a Sabbath of rest unto the land, a

Chapter 5
Refreshing

Exodus 23:12 (KJV)

"Six days thou shalt do thy
and on the seventh day tho
rest; that thine ox and thine
rest, and the son of thy har
and the stranger, may be refr

God Almighty, who form
earth and all its fullness rested
seventh day. This is a b
example of what it means to res
be refreshed.

Rest is a prerequisite
refreshing experience. To
means to restore strength and to

Sabbath for the Lord: thou shalt neither sow thy field, not prune thy vineyard. That which groweth of its own accord of thy harvest thou shalt not reap, neither gather the grapes of thy vine undressed; for it is a year of rest unto the land."

If God wanted the land to have rest every seven years, how much more do we need to rest one day a week? There is a time to work and a time to rest.

In **Romans 15:30-32,** Paul asked the Romans for prayer so he would come to see them with joy in order that they could refresh each other. Joy is contagious and encourages us because the joy of the Lord is our strength.

In **Acts 3:19,** we are instructed to repent and be saved that our sins would be blotted out, when the times of **refreshing shall come from the Lord.** Times of refreshing come from repenting and abiding in the presence of the Lord.

Psalm 16:11 (KJV)

"Thou wilt shew me the path of life; in thy presence is fullness of joy; at thy right hand there are pleasures forevermore."

When the Lord forgives us of our sin, he forgets about them. He blots out our sins. So, if you start to get into condemnation concerning some sin you have committed, say, "No, Jesus has forgiven me and I am the righteousness of God in Christ. I have been redeemed and cleansed from every sin." Then, enter into the joy of the Lord and be refreshed spirit, soul, and body. Hallelujah!

There was a time in my life when the enemy had convinced me that my sins were too great for the Lord to forgive me. The Devil is a liar and the father of all lies. I repented to the Lord that I had believed that lie. When God told me the blood of Jesus was enough to forgive me of my sins, I was no longer deceived. My refreshing came from the Lord that day and every time I reflect on that moment, another refreshing comes from the Lord.

Can you name what refreshes you the most when you are thirsty, tired and dry? My first thought is enjoying the refreshing beauty and melodic sounds of a waterfall.

When the water cascades down the rocks and hills, it is not only majestic and powerful but restful and relaxing to me. A waterfall can be refreshing for us spirit, soul and body.

We read in **Revelation 22:1-2** about a river that flows from the throne of God. It is pure and clear as crystal. In the midst and on either side of the river is the tree of life which is for the healing of the nations.

Isaiah 41:17-18 (KJV)

"When the poor and needy seek water, and there is none, and their tongue faileth for thirst, I the Lord will hear them, I the God of Israel will not forsake them. I will open rivers in high places, and fountains in the midst of the valleys; I will make the wilderness a pool of water, and the dry land springs of water."

Rivers and fountains of water are abundant refreshing gifts from the God of Israel. The Lord refreshes all of us because we are all his favorites.

We are refreshed to know that we are the apple of God's eye and the center of His love. We are refreshed to know that God loves us so much that he even counts the hairs on our head.

Let us pray:

Dear Heavenly Father,

With joy, we draw water from the wells of salvation. We are refreshed in your presence. Thank you for the river of life that flows from your throne.

We desire to come into the water, not just ankle deep, not just knee deep, but all the way in to enjoy the abundant life that you have given to us through your precious son, Jesus Christ.

As refreshing as a waterfall or as anything else we may encounter may be, there is none like YOU, oh Lord, our strength and our redeemer.

You are #1 in our lives. In your presence is fullness of joy. The refreshing that comes from you Father, Son and Holy Spirit endures and sustains us as we walk this pilgrim way.

Thank you so much for our redemption, for reconciling us to you, for making us righteous through Jesus Christ, for giving us the reasons to rejoice, and for refreshing us in your presence.

Be glorified and be magnified in our lives Lord. May your anointing break any yoke of bondage in our lives. May your anointing fill us with the ability to function. We love you. We praise you. Lord, there is none like you both now and forevermore. In Jesus' name, Amen.